ENGLISCH FÜR KINDER

READ ENGLISH WITH ZIGZAG -1

ISBN: 978-1-914911-18-7

www.zigzagenglish.co.uk

ZIGZAG ENGLISH

OUR BOOKS FOR CHILDREN
www.zigzagenglish.co.uk

Our bilingual books for young children. Funny stories in simple, useful everyday English, with colour photos.
English with Tony -1- Tony moves house
English with Tony -2- Tony is happy
English with Tony -3- Tony's Christmas
English with Tony -4- Tony's holiday
My Best Friend

Our coursebook for child beginners (age 7 to 11)
English for Children - 1st Coursebook (Essential vocabulary and grammar for beginners)

Our series of dialogue books for beginners (for beginners aged 7 - 11). With word lists, comprehension questions, speaking tasks and more.
I Speak English Too! - 1
I Speak English Too! - 2

Our series of reading and comprehension books for beginners (for beginners aged 7 - 11). With word lists, comprehension questions and more.
Read English with Zigzag - 1
Read English with Zigzag - 2
Read English with Zigzag - 3
Read English with Zigzag 1, 2 and 3
        Audiobook - Books 1 + 2 (Audible)

The Learn English Activity Book for Children *(A1 - A2, elementary). (Recommended for children in early secondary school.)*

Our series of reading and comprehension books for children at elementary level (recommended for ages 10 - 13). With word lists, comprehension and discussion questions and lots of language activities.
Read English with Ben - 1
Read English with Ben - 2
Read English with Ben – 3

Our series of reading and discussion books (with writing tasks) for *children at secondary school, A2 - B1*
I Live in a Castle – Book 1 – The Choice
I Live in a Castle – Book 2 – The New Me

The Speak English, Read English, Write English Activity Books – *3 books from A1 to B2, for older children and adults.*

Our non-fiction book with language activities
Learn English with Fun Facts! – A2 – B2

English Dialogues for Secondary School – for ages 11 to 17, A2 – B2

OUR BOOKS FOR ADULTS

Our 3 Grammar books with grammar-focused dialogues
Learn English Grammar through Conversation – A1, A2 and B1

Our Dialogue books for adults (with vocabulary lists and comprehension questions)
50 very Easy Everyday English Dialogues (A2)
50 Easy Everyday English Dialogues (A2 - B1)
50 Intermediate Everyday English Dialogues (B1 - B2)
50 more Intermediate Everyday English Dialogues (B1 - B2)
40 Advanced Everyday English Dialogues (B2 – C1)
40 Intermediate Business English Dialogues (B1 - B2)
40 Advanced Business English Dialogues (B2 - C1)

Our activity books for adults and older children
The Speak English, Read English, Write English Activity Books – 3 books, for A1 - A2, A2 - B1 and B1 – B2.

Our non-fiction book with language activities
Learn English with Fun Facts! – A2 – B2

Contents

Die Ziele dieser Buchreihe sind:

1.   Eine unterhaltsame und lustige Lektüre zu sein.
2.   Ihrem Kind das Vertrauen zu geben, Englisch zu lesen.
3.   Ihrem Kind Schlüsselwörter und -sätze beizubringen. Die Bücher führen diese ein, wiederholen sie und bauen sie nach und nach auf, um das Verständnis Ihres Kindes für die englische Sprache zu erweitern.
4.   Ihrem Kind auf einfache Weise die Grundlagen in englischer Grammatik beizubringen.

Wie Sie diese Buchreihe verwenden können:

1.   Vielleicht kann Ihr Kind die Bücher schon ohne Hilfe lesen. Das ist großartig! Aber wenn Sie Englisch sprechen, können Sie ihm bei der Aussprache helfen, indem Sie es ermutigen, Ihnen einige Kapitel laut vorzulesen. **Die Bücher 1 und 2 sind auch als Hörbuch erhältlich.**
2.   In jedem Buch gibt es Vokabellisten, die Sie verwenden können, um Ihrem Kind beim Lernen der neuen Wörter zu helfen.
3.   Es gibt Verständnisfragen, mit Antworten am Ende jedes Buches. Sie können natürlich weitere Fragen hinzufügen und Gespräche über die Geschichte führen.
4.   Es gibt weitere sprachliche Aktivitäten, die Ihrem Kind beim Erlernen von Wortschatz und Grammatik helfen.

Was noch? Wie geht es weiter?

1.   Unsere Reihe mit einfachen Dialogen - **I Speak English Too!** - ist für Eltern gedacht, die ihrem Kind helfen wollen, Englisch zu sprechen. Sie ist ideal für Eltern und Kind, oder für zwei Kinder die gemeinsam lesen und sprechen möchten. Buch 1 beginnt mit den Grundlagen, indem es Schlüsselwörter und -sätze einführt und dann vertieft, sodass Ihr Kind schnelle Fortschritte macht. Schon nach wenigen Lektionen wird Ihr Kind kleine Dialoge auf Englisch mit Ihnen führen können.
2.   Das Lesen von Büchern auf Englisch - egal wie einfach sie sind - macht einen großen Unterschied. Wir empfehlen auch, einfache Fernsehserien für Kinder anzuschauen. Auch wenn sie für englische Muttersprachler konzipiert sind, die etwas jünger sind als Ihr Kind. Auch Hörbücher eignen sich hervorragend, vor allem kurz vor dem Schlafengehen (das hilft dem Kind, die neue Sprache zu beizubehalten). Erwarten Sie nicht, dass Ihr Kind alles sofort versteht - Hörbücher können

immer wieder angehört werden, und Ihr Kind wird jedes Mal mehr verstehen.

3.   Es ist aufregend zu sehen, wie schnell Ihr Kind Fortschritte in einer neuen Sprache macht. Viel Glück und viel Spaß!

Early morning at Zigzag's house

1 I'm Zigzag

Hello! My name's Zigzag. Yes, Zigzag. My name's Zigzag.

I'm six. And I'm a tiger. I'm not a cat. No, I'm not a big cat. I'm a tiger. I'm a small tiger.

What's your name? Are you a tiger? No? Are you a boy? Are you a girl? Are you big or small?

How old are you? Are you eight or nine? Or ten or eleven? I'm six.

I like big boys and girls. And I like small girls and boys.

I like **chicken** and **cheese**. And I like **cat food**. But I'm not a cat. No, I'm not. I'm a tiger.

I'm **busy today**. I'm very busy. I'm very, very busy. Are you busy?

I have to go now, because I'm busy. Can I see you **tomorrow**? Please? Please, please, please, please, please? Yes? Thank you!

Goodbye! See you tomorrow!

Vocabulary

- chicken   Huhn
- cheese   Käse
- cat food   Katzenfutter
- busy   beschäftigt
- today   heute
- tomorrow   morgen

2 Poppy

Poppy is eight. She lives in a nice house in Cambridge. Cambridge is a small **city** in England.

Poppy **lives** with her mum and dad. She has a **little** brother. His name is Adam. He's four. She doesn't have any sisters. But she has two pets – a dog and a cat.

Her cat is called Zigzag. He's **really** big. He **looks like** a little tiger. Her dog is called Pam. She's **quite** big too. She's black and white.

Poppy likes playing with her cat and her dog. And she likes playing with her friends, **too**.

Questions:
1. *Where does Poppy live?*
2. *How old is Adam?*
3. *How many pets does Poppy have?*

Vocabulary
- city   Stadt
- to live   leben
- little   klein
- really   wirklich
- to look like aussehen wie
- quite   ziemlich
- too   auch

3 How many animals do you know?

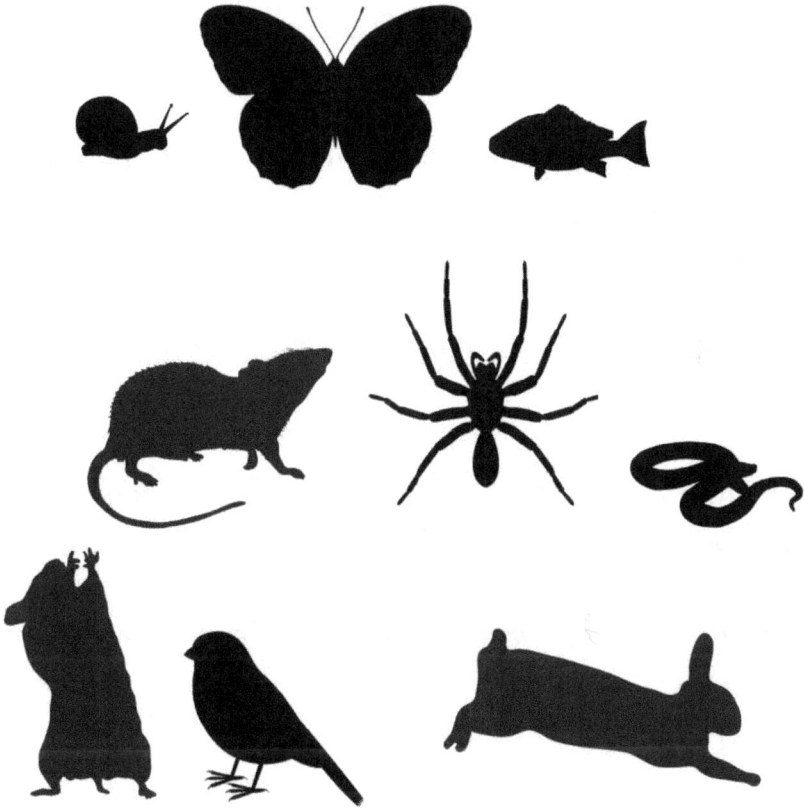

Where is the: hamster, butterfly, spider, rabbit, snail, fish, rat, bird and snake?

4 Pam's a dog

Hello! Hello everyone! I'm Zigzag. My name's Zigzag. What's your name? Is your name Anne? No? Is it Mark? No? What IS your name? How old are you? I'm six!

This is my friend. This is my friend Pam. Pam is a dog. I'm a tiger, **but** Pam's a dog. I'm a small tiger, and Pam is a big dog. I AM NOT A CAT!

I like Pam. I don't like dogs, but I like Pam. Pam is a good dog.

Do you like dogs? Do you like dogs and tigers? Or do you like snakes and spiders?

I'm very **hungry**. I want to **eat** cat food. Pam is hungry too. Pam wants to eat dog food. Cat food is **nice**, but dog food is **horrible**. **Yuck**!

Vocabulary

- but   aber
- hungry   hungrig
- to eat   essen
- nice   gut
- horrible   furchtbar
- yuck   igitt

5 Do you have a pet?

Do you have a hamster or a rabbit? A fish or a bird? A rat or a snake?

Or do you have a cat or a dog? Which is **better**? You **choose**!

CAT or DOG?

Easy to look after?

Friendly?

Intelligent?

Fun?

Funny?

Independent?

Cute?

Beautiful?

Vocabulary

- pet   Haustier
- better   besser
- to choose   wählen
- easy   leicht
- to look after   pflegen
- friendly   freundlich
- fun   Spaß
- funny   lustig
- independent   unabhängig
- cute   süß
- beautiful   schön

6 It's my sofa

Hello! How are you? How are you today? Are you okay? I'm fine. Pam's fine too.

This is my house. My house is big. My house is **lovely**. Do you like my house?

This is my sofa. My sofa is very **comfortable**. I like my sofa. Pam likes my sofa too. But it's MY sofa! Go away, Pam!

This is my **kitchen**. This is my **fridge**. This is my cat food in the fridge.

I'm hungry. I want my cat food!

This is Poppy. Poppy, **give** me my cat food! Please, Poppy!

Thank you!

Vocabulary
- lovely   schön
- comfortable   bequem
- kitchen   Küche
- fridge   Kühlschrank
- to give   geben

7 Adam's hungry

Adam's hungry. He wants to eat:

Ice cream, crisps, biscuits, a doughnut, chocolate and sweets.

His mum wants him to eat:

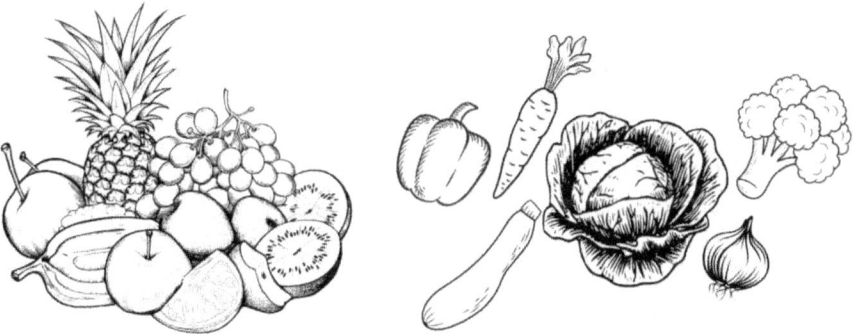

Fruit and vegetables!

Are you hungry? What do *you* want to eat?

8 I don't want to eat cat food

Hello! How are you? I'm okay today. I'm fine.

But I'm hungry. I want to eat **something**. I don't want to eat cat food. And I don't want to eat dog food. Dog food is horrible – yuck!

I want to eat... a spider! I like spiders. I like eating spiders. I like eating big, black spiders! Do you like eating spiders?

Is there a spider in the fridge? No, there's not. Is there a spider in the **garden**? Let's **look for** a spider.

Is this a spider? No, it's not a spider. It's a snail. It's a small snail. What colour is it? It's brown and white. I don't like snails.

Is this a spider? No, it's not. It's a butterfly. It's a beautiful butterfly. What colour is it? It's red, yellow and blue. I like butterflies. Butterflies are nice. They're **pretty**. But I don't like eating butterflies.

I want to eat a spider!

Vocabulary

- something — etwas
- garden — Garten
- to look for — suchen
- pretty — hübsch

9 Poppy goes to school

Poppy goes to school **every day**. No, not every day. Poppy goes to school on Monday, Tuesday, Wednesday, Thursday and Friday.

Adam doesn't go to school. He's too small to go to school. But he goes to **nursery**. Poppy likes going to school, but Adam doesn't like going to nursery. He wants to **stay** at home. He wants to play with the dog in the garden.

Poppy doesn't go to school on Saturday or Sunday. At the **weekend**, Poppy stays at home and plays with her little brother. Sometimes she goes to the park. Sometimes she goes to a friend's house.

Poppy has a **best friend**. She's called Jessica. Jessica is a beautiful name!

Questions:
1. *Does Adam go to school?*
2. *When doesn't Poppy go to school?*
3. *Where does Poppy go at the weekend?*

Vocabulary
- every day   jeden Tag
- nursery   Kindergarten
- to stay   bleiben
- weekend   Wochenende
- best friend   bester Freund

10 Where's my toy?

Hi! Is that you? Is that you **again**? It's nice to see you!

I feel **great**. I'm not hungry. I'm not hungry now. I don't want any cat food. I don't want **another** spider. One spider is **enough**.

Where is my **toy**? I want to play with it.

Is it **on** the **table**? No, it's not.

Is it **under** the sofa? No, it's not.

Is it **behind** the **armchair**? No, it's not.

Where is it? Oh, there it is. It's **next to** the television.

Pam, do you want to play with me? No, she doesn't want to play.

Poppy, do you want to play with me? No, she doesn't.

Adam, do you want to play? Adam? Where are you?

Yes! Yes! Adam wants to play. He wants to play with me! I love you, Adam!

Vocabulary

- again   wieder
- great   großartig
- another   eine weitere
- enough   genug
- toy   Spielzeug
- on   auf
- table   Tisch
- under   unter
- behind   hinter
- armchair   Sessel
- next to   neben

11 School

Poppy and Jessica **walk** to school with Jessica's mum.

Their school is quite big. There are three hundred and fifty children at the school. There are twenty-five children in Poppy's class and twenty-six children in Jessica's class. Jessica's class is bigger than Poppy's.

Poppy's teacher is called Mrs Rice. She's nice. Poppy likes her - most of the time!

Poppy likes **learning** English, but she doesn't like **maths**. Maths is fun, but Poppy doesn't like it. She's bad at maths, but she's very good at English. Poppy likes **break times** best. Sometimes Poppy and her friends play football. Sometimes they **chat**.

On Thursdays, Poppy takes her **swimming things** to school. All the children in her class go swimming at the big **swimming pool** near their school. Everyone loves swimming. Thursday is the best day of the week.

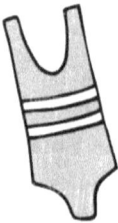

Questions:
  1. *Does Poppy go to school **by car**?*

2. *How big is Poppy's school?*
3. *Does Poppy like maths lessons best?*

Vocabulary

• to walk	zu Fuß gehen
• to learn	lernen
• maths	Mathe
• break time	Pause
• to chat	plaudern
• swimming things	Badesachen
• swimming pool	Schwimmbad
• by car	mit dem Auto

12 It's not my fault

Oh dear. **I'm sorry**. I'm really sorry, Adam.

Does it hurt, Adam?

I'm sorry. But **it's not my fault**. It's really not my fault, is it Adam? It's your fault, isn't it Adam?

Adam is **sad**. Adam has to go to the **doctor's**.

But I want to play. Where's my toy now? Poppy? Do you want to play with me?

Please play with me Poppy! Why not? Why are you **angry**? Why are you angry with me?

I'm sad now. I'm **tired**. I'm hungry. I'm really hungry. I want my cat food!

Vocabulary
- I'm sorry   es tut mir leid
- does it hurt?   tut es weh?
- it's not my fault   es ist nicht meine Schuld
- sad   traurig
- doctor   Arzt
- angry   wütend
- tired   müde

13 At the doctor's

Adam has to go to the doctor's today. Poppy goes with him.

The doctor looks at Adam's hand. His **left** hand. There's a **scratch** on his hand.

"Is there a cat at home?" asks the doctor.

"Yes", says Adam. "I like the cat, but he doesn't like me!"

The doctor puts a **plaster** on Adam's hand. "It's not a bad scratch," he says. "But be **careful** when you play with that cat. Maybe it's really a tiger?"

Questions:
1. **Who** goes to the doctor's with Adam?
2. Is there a scratch on Adam's **right** hand?
3. What does the doctor put on Adam's hand?

Vocabulary
- left   links
- scratch   Kratzer
- plaster   Pflaster
- careful   vorsichtig
- who   wer
- right   rechts

14 I'm sorry

Hello! How are you? Are you okay?

I'm fine. But Adam's not fine. **Poor** Adam.

Look at Adam's hand. He has a big plaster on his hand. Does your hand hurt, Adam?

His left hand hurts, but his right hand doesn't hurt. His right hand is okay.

Adam, can you play with me? Can you play with me with your right hand? Can you?

He doesn't want to play.

Adam, this is for you. This is a **present** for you.

It's a lovely big black spider.

Because I love you, Adam. And because I'm really sorry.

Vocabulary
- poor   arm
- present   Geschenk

15 Birthday party

Poppy wants to **invite** everyone in her class to her birthday party. But her mum says no. Poppy can invite nine friends.

Poppy chooses Jessica and eight other friends. Choosing's not easy.

Poppy's birthday party is so much fun. She gets lots of presents. The best present is a toy dog that **barks.** It looks just like Pam.

The **chocolate** cake is **enormous**. Chocolate cake is Poppy's favourite.

Everyone sings Happy Birthday. **Some** of the children are very bad **singers**!

The party **games** are great. The best game is Musical **Chairs**. When the music **stops**, you have to **sit** on a chair. But there aren't enough chairs! Jessica **wins** that game.

Then there are **races** in the garden. Adam wins the **egg** and **spoon** race.

Questions:
1. *How big is the birthday cake?*
2. *What do the children have to do when the music stops?*

Vocabulary

- birthday party   Geburtstagsfeier
- to invite   einladen
- to bark   bellen
- chocolate   schokolade
- enormous   riesig
- everyone   alle
- some   einige
- singer   Sänger
- game   Spiel
- chair   Stuhl
- to stop   aufhören
- to sit   sitzen
- to win   gewinnen
- race   Rennen
- egg   Ei
- spoon   Löffel

16 Too many boys and girls

Hi there! Is it your birthday today?

It's Poppy's birthday today. Poppy is nine today.

I don't like birthday parties. They're **noisy**. They're too noisy. There are lots of children. There are too many children.

Pam likes birthday parties. She likes noisy children. She likes eating birthday cake too.

I can't sit on my sofa. There are too many children in the living room! I can't eat my cat food. There are too many children in the kitchen! I can't look for a spider in the garden. That's **right** – there are too many boys and girls there!

Mum and Dad's bedroom is **quiet**. Their bed is quite comfortable.

See you tomorrow…

Vocabulary
- noisy   laut
- right   richtig
- quiet   ruhig

17 Party games

This is Poppy's favourite party game. It's called Musical Statues.

Play some music. Everyone **dances**.

When the music stops, everyone has to **stand still. Completely** still.

If you **move**, you're out of the game.

Play the music again.

The winner is the **last** person left.

Adam's favourite race is the egg and spoon race.

Everyone gets a spoon and an egg.

You have to put the egg in the spoon and run with it.

If you **drop** the egg, you have to **pick it up** and put it back in the spoon.

If you use **real** eggs, this race can get very **messy**!

Vocabulary
- to dance   tanzen
- to stand still   stillstehen
- completely   ganz
- to move   sich bewegen
- last   letzte

- to drop   fallen lassen
- to pick up   aufheben
- real   echt
- messy   chaotisch

18 A very small house

Look at this. It's a house. But it's very, very small.

I don't **understand**. Do you understand?

Who lives in this house? Very, very small **people**?

Where are the small people?

Are they **hiding**? Are they hiding in the yellow toy **box**? Are they hiding under the purple armchair? Are they hiding behind the white **bookcase**?

Is there a very small dog too? And a very small tiger?

I don't understand!

Vocabulary
- to understand   verstehen
- people   Menschen
- to hide   sich verstecken
- box   Kiste
- bookcase   Bücherregal

19 A weekend at the seaside

It's **summer** now. It's hot. It's too hot.

Poppy's **excited**. The family is going **away** for the weekend. They're going to a hotel by the sea.

Poppy packs her swimming things - her green **swimming costume** and her **towel**. Adam packs his red **plastic bucket**.

Pam is going to the seaside too. She's very **happy**. She takes her ball.

Adam puts Zigzag's cat toy in the car.

"Zigzag is a cat!" says Mum. "He can't come!"

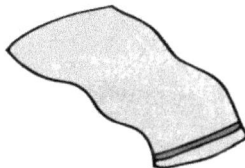

Questions:
1. Is Poppy going to the mountains?
2. What does Pam take with her?
3. Why can't Zigzag come?

Vocabulary

- sea / seaside   Meer
- summer   Sommer
- excited   aufgerecht
- away   weg
- swimming costume   Badeanzug
- towel   Handtuch
- plastic   aus Plastik
- bucket   Eimer
- happy   glücklich

20 The Boss

Hello. Is that you again? I want to tell you a **secret**.

Today is an **important** day.

Today, Mum and Dad and Poppy and Adam and Pam aren't here.

Tomorrow's an important day too. Because tomorrow, Pam and Adam and Poppy and Dad and Mum aren't here.

But I'm here. I'm in the house. Today and tomorrow, this is MY house. I AM THE BOSS.

And this is what I want to do...

Vocabulary
- boss   Chef
- secret   Geheimnis
- important   wichtig

21 Where are they?

in front of?   in?

between?   next to?

        behind?   on?

            under?

22 I want to…

I want to:

Eat all the cat food.

Chase birds in the garden.

Scratch Dad's **special** chair.

Lick the little people in the **doll's house**.

Run up and down the **stairs** ten times.

Pull the children's **pictures off** the fridge.

Bite the **next door neighbour**.

Drink water from the toilet.

Go to sleep in Mum and Dad's bed.

PURRRRRRR… That was so much fun.

Vocabulary

- to chase   jagen
- special   besondere
- to lick   lecken
- doll's house   Puppenhaus
- stairs   Treppe
- to pull off   abreißen
- picture   Bild
- to bite   beißen
- next door neighbour   Nachbar von nebenan
- to drink   trinken
- to go to sleep   schlafen gehen

Word Search

```
Z U O I H X V F P X I L D N H
Y D H Y C E N I U E B H W E G
Z U N D E R S T A N D A W I A
G A M E N F B G Q K S E Z G R
F J F U I A T L D A L N P H D
C L P B C H O C O L A T E B E
X Q Z K G Z M F S A V E O O N
S T A I R S O R O S K C P U K
X R N L C Z R I F W U I L R O
M D Q D V O R D A M U B E Q Z
J Z K H Y Z O G E O A B X X A
G J Y C Z M W E S H P C N G Q
V F G R Y S I M L N R C D E Z
S F H M O E F Q X L Q K U O X
S U W X B A L O V E L Y H D Z
```

- It's summer. It's hot. I want to swim in the **s-a**.
- My **n-ighb-ur** has a **l-v-ly g-rd-n**.

- Why is the  in the **fr-d-e**? Because it's hot today.
- Zigzag runs up and down the **st-ir-** all day.
- I don't **und-rst-nd** how to play the **ga-e** of Musical Chairs.
- There are 2 **peo-le** on my **s-f-**! Get off, it's MY **s-f-**!
- What do you want to do **t-m-rr-w**, Zigzag? I want to eat all the cat food!

Antworten

2

1. She lives in Cambridge in England.
2. He's four.
3. She has two pets.

3

snail, butterfly, fish, rat, spider, snake, hamster, bird, rabbit

9

1. No, he doesn't. He goes to nursery.
2. At the weekend (on Saturday and Sunday).
3. She goes to the park or to a friend's house.

11

1. No, she doesn't. She walks to school.
2. It's quite big.
3. No, she doesn't. She likes break times best.

13

1. Poppy does. Poppy goes with him.
2. No, there's not. There's a scratch on his left hand.
3. The doctor puts a plaster on Adam's hand.

15

1. It's enormous.
2. They have to sit on a chair.

19

1. No, she's not. She's going to the seaside.
2. She takes her ball with her.
3. Because he's a cat.

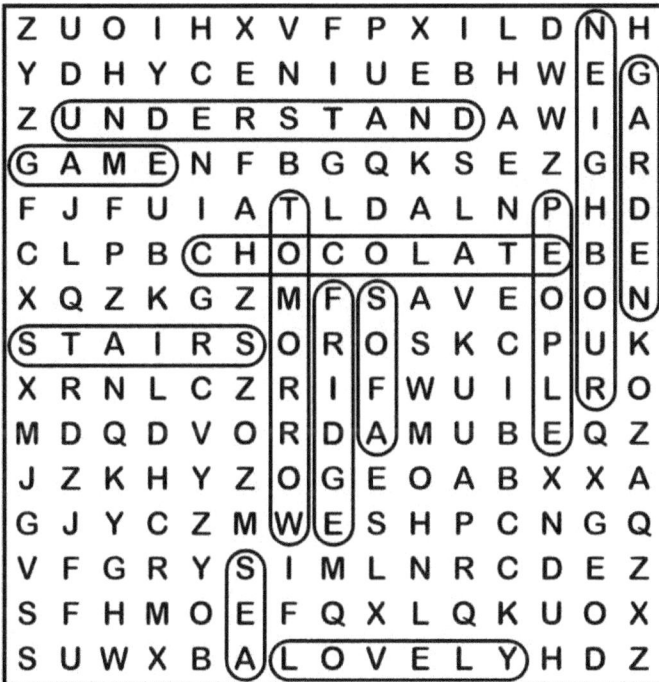

```
Z U O I H X V F P X I L D N H
Y D H Y C E N I U E B H W E G
Z U N D E R S T A N D A W I A
G A M E N F B G Q K S E Z G R
F J F U I A T L D A L N P H D
C L P B C H O C O L A T E B E
X Q Z K G Z M F S A V E O O N
S T A I R S O R O S K C P U K
X R N L C Z R I F W U I L R O
M D Q D V O R D A M U B E Q Z
J Z K H Y Z O G E O A B X X A
G J Y C Z M W E S H P C N G Q
V F G R Y S I M L N R C D E Z
S F H M O E F Q X L Q K U O X
S U W X B A L O V E L Y H D Z
```

Vielen Dank, dass Sie dieses Buch gelesen haben.

Wenn Sie Fragen oder Vorschläge zur Verbesserung des Buches haben, schicken Sie mir bitte eine E-Mail an: lydiawinter.zigzagenglish@gmail.com. Vorschläge für neue Bücher sind auch immer willkommen.

Die Website finden Sie hier: **www.zigzagenglish.co.uk**. Auf dieser Website können Sie und Ihr Kind sich über unsere anderen Bücher für Kinder und Erwachsene informieren und unseren Blog lesen. Sie finden dort auch weitere englischsprachige Aktivitäten.

Ich würde mich freuen, wenn Sie eine Buchrezension hinterlassen. Vielen Dank!

Hier sind einige Auszüge aus unseren anderen Büchern für Kinder, die anfangen, Englisch zu lernen:

5 Where is Poppy?

Hi there!

Can I **ask you a question**?

Where is Poppy? Why isn't she here? Where does she go every day?

Is she hiding in the house?

Is she outside, in the garden?

Do you know where she is?

I'm looking for Poppy. I'm looking for her **downstairs**, in the living-room and the kitchen. And I'm looking for her upstairs, in the bedrooms and the bathroom.

I'm looking for her **inside**, and I'm looking for her outside.

But I can't find her. Why not? Please **help** me find her!

6B

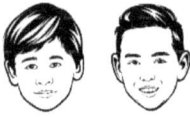

Jack: I really want a dog, Sam.

Sam: Don't you have a cat?

Jack: Yes, I do. I like my cat, but I want a dog too.

Sam: Dogs are nice, but they're very **messy**.

Jack: Cats aren't messy. But they're a bit boring.

Sam: Cats are beautiful. I want a cat, but my dad doesn't want one.

Jack: Does your mum want a cat?

Sam: Yes, she does. She likes cats a lot. But my dad really doesn't like them.

Jack: Does your brother like cats **or** dogs?

Sam: He likes **snakes**.

Jack: Snakes? I **hate** snakes!

CHOOSE!

You can't always have everything you want.
Sometimes you have to choose.
So what do you choose?

- Ice cream or chocolate?
- A hamster or a rabbit?
- Homework or **housework**?
- A holiday at the beach or a skiing holiday?
- One very good friend or three good friends?
- Football or swimming?
- A green bedroom or a white bedroom?
- Autumn or spring?
- Chinese food or Italian food?
- Very hot **weather** or very cold weather?
- Orange juice or a milkshake?

www.ingramcontent.com/pod-product-compliance
Lightning Source LLC
LaVergne TN
LVHW051205080426
835508LV00021B/2813